DEADPAN

DEADPAN

JAMES NORCLIFFE

OTAGO UNIVERSITY PRESS
Te Whare Tā o Te Wānanga o Ōtākou

For Elisabeth and Alejandro

Published by Otago University Press
Level 1, 398 Cumberland Street
Dunedin, New Zealand
university.press@otago.ac.nz
www.otago.ac.nz/press

First published 2019
Copyright © James Norcliffe

Editor: Emma Neale
Design/layout: Fiona Moffat

Cover: Buster Keaton in a scene from the 1922 silent film *Cops*;
Ton Weerayut/Shutterstock.com

Printed in China through Asia Pacific Offset

CONTENTS

PART THREE: TRUMPET VINE

PART FOUR: TELEGRAPH ROAD

PART FIVE: FIVE TRAVELLERS IN A SMALL FORD

Author's preface

Deadpan: Of saying something amusing while affecting a serious manner

While *Deadpan* takes its titles from one of the poems, the word itself is not a bad description of the overall voice or manner of so many of my poems, not only in this but in previous collections as well.

It could be argued, and it has been, that this deadpan manner is a defensive mechanism, a distancing device, and I have no real quarrel with this. Dry ambiguity was very much part of my family background, especially from my north-of-England paternal grandfather and great-grandfather, who were both important fixtures in my childhood. My father inherited the gift – or curse – as have I, in turn passing it on to my son and daughter. It is a curse because at its worst it privileges reticence over passion, and prefers opacity to transparency, jokes to engagement. On the other hand it is useful for the kind of poetry I try to write and like to read: allusive, elusive, wry and surprising.

Ambiguity in language was also found on my maternal side. I had grandparents and a team of uncles and aunts I could barely understand because of their broad and rapid accents: Lallans Scots. This could be the source of a predilection towards incomprehensibility at times.

When I was small the Queen toured New Zealand following her coronation. I waved my flag and received my coronation medal. At the time we were going to be the new Elizabethans; the Queen was *Gloriana* reinvented; Hillary and Tensing had conquered Everest.

Nobody talks much about the new Elizabethans now – Britten's opera has been mothballed and God knows where the royal barge is. My disposition still prefers the old Elizabethans. I like their cynicism, especially towards mortality and life's fleeting, transitory nature. Macbeth's brief candle, Jaques' stage and just about all of *Hamlet*. The famous gravedigger scene where the skull of the court jester Yorick, whom Hamlet knew well, is unearthed neatly encapsulates the dual attitude: nostalgia and affection for the living Yorick coupled with repulsion for the dead one, wrapped around with a meditation on death.

Giving Yorick a voice not only allowed me to give him a chance to respond and develop the meditation, but also it allowed me to *be* Yorick, or, perhaps more accurately, Yorick's skull. I do like the persona poem and have written many over the years. At first glance, speaking through a persona might appear to be another distancing device, the appropriation of another voice, and of course it is, to an extent. On the other hand, given that what we are is simply a reflection of all that we have experienced, directly or indirectly, the true persona poem is of course an impossibility. You can only keep the costume and the makeup in place for the brief moment of the performance.

When I was not quite so small, perhaps nine or ten, I was kicking around with some older cousins in the Buller (the district, not the river) and they asked me, perhaps teasing, what I wanted to be when I grew up. Quite disingenuously, rather than opting for the known quantities of coal miner, crane operator or racing car driver, I said, 'a pote' (rhymes with goat). They did laugh but, perhaps because they were girls, they laughed at the pronunciation rather than the ambition.

I'm not sure where that particular ambition came from. There were books in our house but not many, and not many poetry books apart from Burns in an elderly edition, a Palgrave, and one of my father's old school anthologies. I don't remember much poetry at primary school although there probably was some. I do remember hymns at the Presbyterian church that amid the dross had the odd thrilling line. Bunyan's 'To Be a Pilgrim' with its great tune and wonderful lines: *come wind, come weather … hobgoblin, nor foul fiend …* was up there, but I didn't see that as poetry then.

When I did come to poetry, as I did at high school with Shakespeare of course, and Keats, Wordsworth and the romantics, I found like-minded friends and we began to explore poetry beyond the classroom. I remember few modern poets and fewer New Zealand poets. These mostly had to wait until university, when the floodgates opened.

As most adolescents do, I began to write poetry at high school. Bad poetry of course, cursed with sentimentality but occasionally redeemed by wit. Later I cringed at the former but was often surprised by the latter. I saw eventually that the poetry I enjoyed most tended towards the playful, the wry, the cryptic: poetry that offered possibilities rather than shutting them down. I did not like shouty poetry, poor-me poetry, poetry that told me stuff and did not want me to argue.

Through marriage to Joan and the arrival of children, poetry remained part of my life. I began to read it in public, overcoming shyness, and found I loved the buzz I got from audience reaction. Gathering courage, I submitted poems to local journals and found they were accepted from time to time.

Unlike most of our friends, we did OE the wrong way round – after children – and when we did 'up sticks' it was not to Earls Court and the rest of Europe, it was to Tianjin in China, where we stayed for two years. While we were there my first book came out through Hard Echo Press, an imprint of Warwick Jordan of Hard to Find Books fame, now in Dunedin, previously in Onehunga. There is something a little wistful in the fact that when my very first book was published, I was 11,000 kilometres from the event.

I remained stoic about this. Deadpan, perhaps.

I like deadpan. It embraces ambiguity, a fusion of opposites. It also embraces uncertainty. Is this serious? How serious? Funny? How funny? Or is it both? It also embraces absurdity and surrealism, two elements I love in literature and introduce in my poems from time to time. It is the porter in *Macbeth* pausing to take a piss while there is that urgent banging at the gate. It is Buster Keaton standing unmoved as the building crashes down on top of him. It is my poker-faced Yorkshire grandfather playing two little dicky birds sitting on the wall.

PART ONE
POOR YORICK

Poor Yorick

1 *Yorick's heart*

Yorick lies on his hospital bed
in his new pyjamas, red
with small yellow aeroplanes.

So cheerful, someone said.

The label scratches the back
of his neck; they have taken
his scissors and shoelaces.

The aeroplanes smelt faintly
of diesel and formaldehyde.

Poor insects, Yorick thought,
picturing the container floor:
dried carapaces, black ants all
dead and scattered like full stops,
silverfish, the dust of wings,
littered in their final bed.

Once they'd throbbed like a heart,
throbbed with something like a heart,

now all dead.

2 Yorick has a problem with personal freshness

He is increasingly depressed by the news.
Summer has given way to summer, has
given way to summer, has given way to summer.

The litter could be petals
or it could be moths:
such desiccation.

Everything he steps on crunches
and behind him the crunch of footsteps.

He can still hear them
after they've stopped,
possibly resting
on their crutches,

keeping their distance,
everything keeping its distance—
the rain, the seasons, memory.

Could it be me? thinks Yorick,
beset by loss,
hoping it wasn't,
suspecting it was.

3 Yorick loses his gibes

There was a time when
with a fig or an orange
or two small pieces of paper,

accompanying himself
with flying fingers
on a squash racquet,

shuffling his soft shoes,
wiggling his ears,
crossing his eyes,

crossing his heart,
blowing his cheeks,
his lips, his nose,

he would jump, stamp
camp it up, vamp:
he could let loose

the giggling puppies,
their scamper, their wag,
their bedraggled laughter …

now they lie out in the sun
wheeze when they rise,
milky-with-cataracts eyes

all remembering gone
long, long before
the hereafter

4 Yorick as beast of burden

They would ride him, as cowboys,
longing for spurs to prick him,
stick it to him, they would yell,
flail their ten-gallon hats
above him and across the prairie
they'd ride him, twist and turn
him until he'd buck them rise above them
knees red raw and sore with carpet burns,
carpet burns all over him

and love them.

5 Yorick contemplates drinking straws for the future

He lays them out
pastel tubes striped:

this one blue
as a summer sky,

this one red
as a rabbit's eye,

this one green
as a memory,

a forgotten leaf
a remembered tree,

this one yellow
as straw can be,

this one brown
as a world to be.

6 Yorick admires the spider lily

To one so long in the soil
such perennial display
is disconcerting.

Nothing dead was ever this blue:
these are the irises of angels,
midnight amethysts,
chalcedony.

They bring him to his knees.
He faces, noses them.

Then the scent of Persephone,
the scent of the earth
tumbled together
unsteady him,
unready him
for his return.

7 Yorick laughs

like a yew berry
like a diagnosis
like an ambassador of grief

like a father
like a mother
like a yawning gulf

like an afterthought
like an embarrassment
like a falling leaf

like an interloper
like a no hoper
like a groping thief

8 Yorick weeps

like a mulberry
like a jelly baby
like a wet summer day

like an oxeye
like a mayfly
like a forgotten castaway

like a dropped stitch
like a sales pitch
like a bad memory

like a wellspring
like a bee sting
like a terrified banshee

like a grindstone
like a headstone
like a gaping cave

like a dull blade
like a muddied spade
like an opened grave

9 Yorick considers the worm

He's heard of your democratic appetite,
little wriggler,
but his gut instinct is not to approve:

through your intestinal tract,
little wriggler,
such traffic on the move.

All that life feeds, feeds life
little shoveller,
come what may,

and while you'll never be his,
little lover,
he will be yours one day.

10 Yorick considers the prince

Raised now to the level of your eyes
I can see those eyes so desperate
in their pity and surmise.

You remember my gibes, I
remember your laughter at my gibes
before this black disguise

wrapped you in perpetual mourning.
Stones rise from the earth like teeth.
The graveyard where the raven flies

is a maw will swallow us all,
re-swallow me. I need not tell you
this, dear prince, it's no surprise

to you for death is your thing, isn't it?
My thing too, but mine was the death of that
tatterdemalion, fun. Yours the death of lies.

11 Yorick considers the cat who may

It is a tricky thing
to tweak a king

dangerous too
dangerous three

He might well laugh
at your tomfoolery

dangerous four
dangerous five

which contaminates
His Majesty

dangerous six
dangerous seven

to give him spectacles
to let him see

dangerous eight
dangerous nine

to polish their lenses
dangerous ten

so dangerously
to set him free.

12 Yorick remembers gambolling

Lambs gambolled,
Yoricks, too,
into lamb
and Yorick stew.

13 *Yorick considers Hamlet's skull*

It is beneath the dissembling flesh,
there where your last laugh
will be fixed forever,
as my grin has been,
and though my
foolscap's long been rotten,
my fleshly face
long forgotten,
it's good to know
despite these
inarticulate jaws
my merry, brown
skull can cause
so loud, so long
and such a revolted laugh
from yours.

PART TWO
SCAN

Scan

Such a tiny finger
so clear there in the phone.
I think of Michelangelo—
God and Adam and point,
putting my own finger
to yours to move your image
from landscape to portrait,
a portrait in black and white,
the profile of a swimmer:
small nose, open mouth, suck,
and you are all there: sex,
arm and leg, thigh, everything
if I were to inspect you
closely, everything for now
except a name, a voice—
yet these like so much else
will come with the imminent
business of birth, of life,
of love and touch and seasons,
as I scroll you back into
landscape, the world about
you waiting, changing even
as you begin to begin.

Night watch

Because your child
could not sleep,
you could not sleep.

Then, when your child
finally slept, because
your child could wake up,
you could not sleep.

And so the night
became heavy.

In that heaviness
you could hear
the breath of trees,
the stretch of ceilings,
the flex of walls.

When at last
your eyes did close,
there was something
at the window,
then an open door,
then a dark lake,

your child
standing there,
open-eyed,
awake.

The last stop before Bethlehem

The bus throbs patiently
as I stand swaying in the aisle.
The only eyes those of the man
at the wheel in his rear-vision
mirror, magnified, disembodied.

The hospital had been less than forthcoming,
but I had got the picture, or at least the frame.
The wheeze of hydraulics opening the door
and I'm so grateful for breath I
murmur my thanks to the driver
for delivering me to this sodium light,
these windows, meters, these muted stars.

There is a wind, too, again the breath
of white noise, the whole city breathing
with its eyes closed, whispering that I
should join it blind-folded on some
ridiculous trust-walk through the dark
alleys and channels of its beating heart.

But there is nothing to trust, really
except to trust people to do their jobs:
surgeons, bus drivers, and the tired woman
leaning in the light behind this glass
doorway who may or may not deliver me
a long black, and should I so desire
another, and an hour or so of her breath.

Black-faced sheep

He had been thrown upon
the ocean like a message
in a bottle and ended up
in a glass-bottomed boat
through which he and his
fellow refugees watched
the sharks gathering as
the food and water ran out.

He spent his days counting
their dark shapes, their teeth,
their gill slits, the number of times
his family had been arrested.
He knew little melody and had
next to no songs, despite the fact
his father's father had once been
an adept on the two-stringed fiddle.

While the others succumbed one
by one to music, mathematics
won the day for him and he
survived to live another life.
Within their hedgerows his days now,
like black-faced sheep, batten on
the green grass of luck. They all look
the same way at any untoward noise.

Route 1003

When the driver remarked
that he was a man of compassion
I decided that his was the best bus.

I liked the way he grasped the wheel
with a measure of insouciance
that belied his words

for he let the bus run idle
until I had aged sufficiently
to make the journey

and he seemed to know the time,
the exact time, for he eased out
into the traffic with a casual

wave to the road as if wishing
it farewell and banks of cars
parted like the Red Sea,

parted in acceptance of
his compassionate presence.

And comforted by signs such as these,
I closed my eyes and wept.

The poets at Makara

gather windswept
beneath angry notices
protesting windmills

they shout at each
other but the wind
rips away their words

hurls their images
seaward where the
crashing waves dash

them onto the rocks
all analogy, all comparison
lost, sucked into a vortex

of wailing snagged
flapping on spinifex
and matagouri until

chastened, defeated
the poets regroup to
find haven in a minivan

drive silently through
green valleys of willow
trees and hydrangeas

green valleys where
arum lilies poke out
their yellow tongues

Hochstetter's frog

Tiny jewelled pawn
all eyes, mouth and legs
half-sprung for jumping.

You could have been a radio star
if the dice hadn't rolled
the radio's way:
eyes closed,
a crooner swaying
in an unseen green tuxedo.

Instead you crouch
in moss and spawn: wet, weak,
eyes wide open,
feet flexed and curled,
primed to leap
compelled to creep
up out of the creek
up and out of the whole
bleak, benighted world.

Naughty boys' island

Not so much an island:
more a grey sandbank
dividing a grey river where
it broadened out between
lines of pollarded tamarisks
just before Brighton.

You had always lived there:
dreamt of crouching among
the reeds, the debris,
the silt-stained plastic bags
and broken bottles; of claiming
your muddy citizenship,

although you were never as
naughty as the river which
wet your stolen cigarettes,
extinguished your matches.
Let me take you to my island
the wicked river whispered.

I'll be waiting here for you when
you have coined those fucking cars,
kicked those letterboxes over
the wicked river lied.
Trust my channels, trust
my current, trust my rushing tide.

Crabmeat on the fifteenth floor

The platters circulate
the terrace, the proffered
legs carapaced in red

with flesh protruding
white, wet with the scent
of the ocean, of sex.

This should be forever:
as if forever tasted
of Riesling and crabmeat,

as if forever lingered
on your fingers long
after the door closed,

long after the elevator
slid silently down
to the brilliant lobby.

Ziziphus

The little jujuba (so desired)
might have retrieved China:

temple-red dates on spiny branches
sweet and mealy in the mouth,

a taste of mist-filled gorges,
gardens of rock, bristle

of black needles clustered
on contorted pines of ink.

But the real world: sun, wind, rain
frost white and brittle on the grass,

seasons of death, seasons of renewal,
a spade and a barrow by the compost.

Mycroft

Because I had no older brother
I was forced to be the oldest son.

I wasn't much cut out for it.
I needed you to blaze the trail,

cut scarves on all the tall trees
I was forever getting lost in,

brainier, better, a dab hand with
an axe or a chainsaw. Compass

in hand you would have strode forth
along roads I couldn't even see

not having an older brother's
clever sense of direction, acuity.

But I puddle along, Mycroft,
solving the odd crime here and

there, trusting I'll grow into you
one day or, saving that, growing big

enough to fit into that Harris tweed
overcoat you left hanging in the closet,

old theatre tickets, bus tickets, lolly
wrappers, but no compass in its pockets.

Silly really, as I never will. And now our old man's gone, does it really matter any more?

other lives

you were the one
gripping the pole
at the deep end

so cold in the rip
the water running
the water streaming
down over your hair
your slicked shoulders

the other lives netted
flopped on the packed
sand white-bellied
gasping in the scrabble
of scuttling claws

then were stowed in
a twitching gunny sack
even as other lives
hovered shrieked and
bickered at the edge of things

or bucked and bowed before
the wind and flying sand
on the dunes you trudged
back over sack in hand

and would not have
had things otherwise

The greengage man

The mornings were bitter, colder than our clothes.
The road clattered with stones, cracked with ice,

and every once in a frightening while the Great Dane named Hamlet
escaped his wooden bars and loped, loped and dropped his jaws.

The dilemma: should you freeze, or should you try to outrun
his stretched legs, close your ears to the rasp of his breath?

Our breath was white, our fingers red with chilblains,
our legs were puny, putty, flimsy as cocksfoot and useless.

He was the colour of the hills, and as large, and when he barked
the thunder echoed in the creeks and gullies. That was winter.

Then spring. Then summer, and with summer the greengage man
and Hamlet, shrunk into his cage, green now, sweet and delicious.

PART THREE
TRUMPET VINE

Trumpet vine

There was that tower
they built on the hill high above you
up by the reservoir,
remember?

The tower that frightened you
so much you wanted to wear
a lead helmet because of
the emanations,

until I pointed out that lead
was probably more dangerous.
You'd be better off chopping
the damn thing down

then taking your axe to the plastic,
the petrol, the asbestos, the 2,4,5-T,
except that you wouldn't have the time,
remember,

or the energy already sapped
by the emanations. Better to
change shape, become a vine
and climb, climb

flamboyantly, climb and smother
foliate and tendril, trumpet vine,
cow itch vine, and flower there,
enjoy the view.

Underwear

Deep in the forest the priests
and the secret police are on patrol.

They are so difficult to see among the black branches
and their scurry cannot easily be heard,

although sometimes, just below the wind
and the dripping rain, the tell-tale snap

of a branch will give them away
so that you know they are there.

Their interest, their fascination is underwear:
your underwear: its stains, secretions

and odours and what it tells the state
of the state of your body, your soul.

This knowledge so excites them their fingers flex with it,
stretch with it to part the foliage, their eyes bright

with the possibility that your underwear will
give you away, deliver you completely to them

and they are grateful to your underwear, so grateful
they express their gratitude in files, in trials, in prayers.

The tennis ball

When I return to the dog, the first thing I see is the teeth.

And then the dog disappears.

But the teeth remain.

Bared.

Bereft of dog.

The bared teeth.

They open wide as if to seize upon the fuzz and flesh of a tennis ball, a tennis ball

I suddenly need as much as I need anything.

The need is so great, I close my eyes, but the teeth remain white in the darkness.

Dog teeth.

Canines.

And then in the darkness: barking.

And beyond the barking the thwack thwack of a tennis ball.

Wet.

Bouncing.

There are times I feel like the egg

These are the times I feel like the egg
you can't make an omelette without breaking.
These are soggy paper-handkerchief days
and forced to walk the arthritic dog
I discover there are no shortcuts
through the suburbs of my malaise.

These are the times I feel like the lamp-post
the animal strains towards so keenly.
The rain though little more than a mist seeps
through me like ink, the ink that flows
thicker than blood, than water, writing
that what you sow is what you'll reap

and other cheap lessons from the people
who pass them down from pillar to post
and who pass me by with scurrying legs
hurrying their own bedraggled beagles
hurrying homewards eyes averted
for their bitter tea and scrambled eggs.

Three times upon a time

Three times upon a time she told me that she loved me.

The first time upon a time was in a lilac hedge under stars sprinkled like talcum. Embraced by leaves we embraced each other and in that embrace she murmured the words.

The second time upon a time was frolicking in a field where wrapped around with grass we wrapped around each other and in that wrapping she whispered the words.

The third time upon a time was in the ocean. As white horses crashed around us and gripped by an undertow we gripped each other and although the salt and surf all but drowned her words I understood clearly what she was attempting to say.

And did we live happily ever after?

We planted a lilac hedge and monthly clipped the heart-shaped leaves.

We grew a lawn and mowed it weekly.

We never visited the ocean.

Precious McKenzie lifts himself

Eyes squeezed shut, Precious McKenzie
hooks his thumbs beneath his armpits and lifts.

The grass grows and moves in the wind.
The clouds, white powder, drift across the heavy sky.

Eyes now open, Precious gauges their height.
His diaphragm dilates. He is inspired.

The bar that is gravity presses on his chest,
the weight of the sky forces him down.

But it is not enough, Precious believes.
And that belief so clenches, so grips his will

he will hoist himself beyond the earth,
hold himself aloft for one eternal moment

before dumping himself down again so violently,
so heavily all the birds will scatter like applause.

The madness of crowds

The only shells on the beach are the high-priced shells on the stall tables. High-priced shells sheltered by canvas. The beach itself cannot be seen. Bodies. You manoeuvre gingerly between them and make your way to the water. Bodies. You make your way between them. Legs. Arms. Heads covered in towels. There is no delineation between the sandline and the waterline because of the bodies. Bodies massed at the unseen border. Two worlds merged into one. As you move into the water the bodies grow shorter, lose legs, lose thighs, waists, midriffs. As you move farther out the bodies become disembodied. Lose chests, breasts, shoulders. Now just heads neckdeep in water. Heads and beach balls. Bodyless beachballs bobbing among the bodied heads. Now you must tiptoe and bounce to keep your head above the water, now visible beyond the heads, beyond the beachballs. Somewhere beyond these there is water moving, heaving water. Somewhere beyond is the sea. Somewhere beyond the sea are continents, bodies.

M. Hulot and the canary

It's a great scene:
M. Hulot arranging the sunlight
so that the canary will sing.

How the light splashes over Montmartre!
M. Hulot swings the casement
to catch it, to fill the glass to dazzling

and in that dazzle the canary glows
like a golden throstle and sings.

The window M. Hulot sees
is an on-off switch, a yes-sing no-sing
light-swing shade-swing thing
enough to make the canary mechanical—
and M. Hulot (bless him) divine, a king.

Deadpan

Old stone face
doesn't allow a flicker
stands stolid
even as the world collapses.

Old flat hat
landing place for a spade
looks left
right straight ahead.

Monsieur Grimface
doesn't even express a fart
a grimace
as timbers splinter

windows shatter
joists members dismember
stands instead
unblinking in falling dust.

Old deadpan
unsurprised by life death
the empty
coffee pot at breakfast

Old Banjo
framed fretted
no tuning pegs
no strings

Control tower

Roger desired a control tower.

Joanne saw through him immediately.

In the garden, said Roger.

No, said Joanne.

It would be nice, Roger insisted, positioned between the *Cercis Forest Pansy* and the *Cornus Eddie's White Wonder*.

It would clash.

It would have a certain majesty. A garden sculpture. It would out-sculpture all other garden sculptures, but slender, towering.

No, said Joanne.

It would make a statement, said Roger. It would have stature, height, lights.

I have read Freud, said Joanne.

Red for port, green for starboard, and blue for the ineffable sadness of the world, said Roger.

No colours, said Joanne.

And it would be useful, said Roger, for the control of air traffic.

We don't have air traffic, said Joanne, but I do believe now we're really getting to the nub of it.

There is air traffic, said Roger. Lights high in the sky, vapour trails like ribbons to paradise.

You don't want to control ribbons or vapour, said Joanne. Let them be.

It would make a statement, said Roger.

No, said Joanne. No control tower.

But, said Roger.

No buts, said Joanne. No colours. No traffic. No lights. No tower.

Pool

Be mindful of slippery surfaces:
if you lose your footing you
may not be able to find it again.

Remember that the pool is
shallower than you think: blue
is as deceptive as it is seductive.

If you must run, run very slowly.
Imagine yourself in slow motion
and then become your imagination.

Observe the operating hours. Swimming
alone and at night-time can lead to
misguided thoughts and fantasies:

the water can become the ocean;
the shiny tiles that circumscribe you
can disappear and so can you,

a fate you richly deserve for
swimming in darkness, shattering
the moon, scattering stars.

We remind you, finally, that your key
is not transferable: only authorised bodies
are permitted. This key legitimises yours.

Thank you & Sincerely,
Pool Committee

He had this thing

He had this thing about flies.

It started with the compound eyes so perfectly compartmentalised. He saw them as textured goggles with thousands of three-dimensional pixels. Hell's angels. Goggles and eyes upon eyes. He obsessed how they could capture him in reverse micro images which they would reassemble to form fly-pictures, fly's-eye views of him. Even as they were flying.

She tried to ignore it.

Even as they were whining and zigzagging erratically across the room.

When he swung at them they accelerated and the whine became angry.

Their anger angered him.

She told him to ignore them.

They were wearing goggle-like fly masks hiding their fly identities.

She told him to stop it.

And when they were still, nothing improved.

Their standing on vertical surfaces was improbably perverse, but real.

Their ability to walk upside down on the ceiling even more so.

She told him to shut the screen door.

And he hated their thoraxes almost as much as he hated the word thorax. When he said the word, it sounded like dried coffee grounds in his mouth. Thorax. Thorax.

And their brown, brittle exoskeletons. Unsoft. Unfleshy. Unwarm.

Go for a walk, she said. They're getting to you.

They vomit, he said. Digest, then vomit and digest again.

Think of something else, she said.

He tried.

Eggs.

More eggs.

Maggots.

The confession

It always gets back, officer, to that moment when crime is possible;
consequence-free crime, the possibility we rarely expect to see on offer,
the moment our ethical self, our superego if you will, officer, spontaneously
combusts.

These hot, hot days when the tar bubbles on the road, the footpath, the soles of your
shoes stick momentarily with a faint squish as you run. So hot, the air swells with
the crack of cicadas, the crackle of broom pods snapping.

It is the last day of this world, officer. The next day you leave. Your life is in
cartons, strapped, labelled, waiting for dispatch.

We are talking crime, officer, not sin. A sound, not noise.

We are talking of a moment it is possible. And it is possible. So you act.

And the moment lasts forever.

Pursued by crabs

I can still see the sea: site of my stupidity, the far horizon line.

All day the tide had sculpted sand into tiny wet dunes punctured with holes
as round and as wide as if they were made with Staedtler pencils by literate crabs
who crouched within, poised to take the evidence.

Beyond the dunes: the grey water where the bigamists were sporting, frolicking,
foolishly believing they couldn't be identified from the shore.

But I was taking notes.

The crabs were taking notes.

I had the bigamists' number, but the crabs had mine.

Through binoculars, I looked to the horizon, but the crabs took a sideways view,
preferring joy to judgement.

And as one they emerged from their pencil holes, lifted their pincers, made ready
to scuttle, their small black eyes full stops to end my sentence.

Dear Messrs Smith & Wesson

I have located you and your dream
in my shoulder holster.
Do you mind if I join you?

Do you mind if I draw you
with your sideburns just a little
singed and powder-burnt?

Somehow the dream has shifted
from the dusty main street,
the verandas and hitching posts

to asphalt freeways, to black SUVs.
The rain has turned to hail,
sunshine to sodium and neon.

I was a stakeholder in your dream,
dear Smith, dear Wesson, but
you've made my stake obsolete,

though I guess it was ever useless,
never fitting in the glovebox, having
no heft in the cradle of my hand.

You must know that heroes have gone
the way of horses, and the noise
in the distance is not tomorrow any more.

PART FOUR
TELEGRAPH ROAD

Telegraph Road

I was driving down Telegraph Road
through the static on the car radio,

lines of tall pines on either side
and power poles on the verge.

Behind these stretched flat paddocks
long-necked alpacas browsed

as if some innovative farmer
had crossed his sheep with giraffes.

This was where it all started, I thought,
looking for the telltale hiccough

where a pine hedge had played
hopscotch and jumped to one side

or sidestepped like a running back,
but it wasn't where I thought it was,

or I missed it because of the stock
ahead on the road, Holstein Friesians

I guessed, black blotched with white
or white blotched with black, ideal

metaphors really with graceful swinging
backsides and gently twitching tails being

switched along by three farmers in dayglo
jackets from one side of the fault line

to the other, from the past of one
paddock to the future of another

so slowly it seemed to take forever
as the static swirled about me

and the engine idled. You might
ruminate, I murmured, but I bet

you don't even remember.
I closed my eyes: cattle, sheep,

giraffes, alpacas. Nothing lasts,
they murmured. Get used to it.

Wallet

She did not remember where she'd dropped her wallet
and discovered she had lost herself,

but, then, she was forever shedding things:
flats, friends, lovers. She was (I always felt) deciduous

and decidedly so. Now, returning to the empty
forest she retraced her steps, although there was little there

to find except turning leaves soon to drop and gather
and the detritus of a world she no longer had purchase on:

yellowing paper, crumpled cans, a lost left shoe (pink)
and a moon she'd never noticed, white between the branches.

But no wallet, though it was probably there somewhere in the shadows
of the tall trunks, along with her few banknotes, her cards, herself.

scrim

through scrim the world
is filtered brown and smells
of flax and coconuts

masked and divided
between the kidnapped
and the kidnappers

what were once buildings
crouch in their sorrow
suffering the cold music

of wind tugging
and flapping at
the sheeting

all is crosshatched
an enlarged stamp
from an undelivered letter

the address smudged
the ink running
the ransom long forgotten

Site content

Ignoring the warning I stepped
under the barrier and straightened.

Of course there was no real danger
in loose gravel and splintered wood.

Besides there was silence and while
no noise is bad noise I was still comforted.

What had been hazardous was long gone:
the trees, the animals (their teeth and stripes),

the tall chimneys, the tiles, the wind vanes,
the architraves and all the howling at the moon.

Long gone. Like the moon itself, long gone.

Geographies

1 ocean

you breathe in slowly
and slowly breathe out

the moon in your eyes
salt on your flesh

I want to tell you
about the visitor

the one with the
official clipboard

a biro and a litany
of disquieting facts

but you would only laugh
moonstruck before

striking out on that rippling
path that arrows towards

the horizon
your backstroke

shiny
easy

2 *littoral*

this is the line
between us

the line that marks
where you start
and I begin
or I start
and you begin

it is the sweetest
disputed territory

such sweet depository
of gifts, offerings

3 *land*

it's where we're coming into once we can get these clouds out of our eyes
somewhere far below us spread out and crumpled:
a table cloth splattered with food-stains yet shining with cutlery
there's water too but don't be deceived by it although it is so very level, so very
seductive

it's where we came from, remember?
when we were children
before we were we

children, remember?
shading our eyes once
looking up at the sky

4 the harbour

Beyond the window, beyond the waxeyes and the lancewood, the harbour lies.
Grey today, its ever-shifting colours, moods and tides are beautiful, deceptive.
The hills, too, between which it stretches, are at once seasonal and constant.

The little lighthouse, like a lollipop with its red and white livery, sits on its rock.
Here and there yachts lean to a wind I cannot see or feel. There will be spume
and a cold rushing as they pitch and jibe, but from here they scarcely seem to
move.

Yesterday, I took the ferry to the port. The sea was rough and the catamaran
bucked and thwacked making the older children laugh and the dogs whimper.
It's a short crossing, a flurry and then it's over, nothing to write home about really.

All the same, there is some place between here and there, then and now, I cannot
quite inhabit, although it inhabits me. Inhibits me too, to be mildly playful.
There is the calm of distance and the chaos of intimacy, grass moving on the hills
becomes mere colour.

There is the road, of course, that follows the harbour and climbs the hill. You
drive it each day to the city where you continue your vigil. You at once take me
with you and disappear from me. Distance. *Gestalt.* Waves. Things are and cannot
be seen

as the port cannot be seen from the window because of the huge black
macrocarpas the German planted. The port is there because I can hear it. Sound
travels across water: the beep-beep of reversing trucks, piles being driven,
bumps, thuds, all

the agencies of industry, of distraction. Across the harbour, on top of Sugarloaf is
a tower, and below the tower the all but unseen pass winds up the hill to a vee in
the ridge and disappears; yet another disappearing act. It is an odd paradox that

at night the road is more clearly visible. The headlights become small stars moving up and down the hillside, small anonymous stars, one of which, these nights, will be you. Until your return, the harbour lies between us, a black mirror, moving, still.

Helios

and the voice in the darkness
asked *Are you sleeping, Helios?*

or it may have asked
What are you seeking, Helios?

and I who was not Helios
and who had been sleeping

answered
Not now

a good answer, I think
to either question

for the voice
did not reply

Waiting for the mulberry

once at a faraway time
it came all the way from Pakistan:

a leaf as heart-shaped
as the Vale of Kashmir

from hemisphere
to hemisphere.

Its fruit a drupe:
a fleshy catkin,

a juicy lip-staining
taste explosion.

These winter birds
fossicking among the myrtle's

dried berries, like old men
lost among the romantic fiction,

have no idea
what's going to hit them

and nor do we
having no intention

of going round and around
although we do, although we do,

while losing traction
while losing traction.

She moved through the silence

At first it was welcome
lapping on her shore,
like a cleansing foam
cool and full of grace;

the quiet wind from
the east calmed her,
ruffled her hair,
made her beautiful.

But the silence grew
icy, sharp-edged,
snagging at her. She felt
its rip, its undertow.

Then when she
moved through
the deeper silence,
the darker silence,

it clutched at her,
froze her to the core,
whispering cruel nothing
into her ear. And there

she would be bound
for days until he deigned
to speak again, asking
for the pepper perhaps,

or for the salt.

Leaves

There is too much nothing here ... –Derek Walcott

Leaf litter upon leaf litter,
dry, slippery, the now-dead
lingering on the forest floor.

There was that question I needed
to ask, there were so many things
I needed to say, but I could not

for your eyes were filled with layers
of leaves before you turned away.
All I wanted was rain, I wanted

the shine of water on broadleaf,
green leaf, the shine and sheen
of it, the clean wet patter of it,

but there was no rain, only
a dry wind and leaves, dead leaves,
and all the things I couldn't say.

Invasion

I'm frightened of the rust,
spores catching the wind,
their all but invisible filaments
billowing as the light thickens.

The market for mulching machines
will soar, chips will fly
parks and gardens whine
as the piles rise. So what

if the worst case scenario is
also the best case scenario,
the green spotted with yellow,
the brown dropping to the ground?

Pine pollen dusts the pond
even as the trees die. Such
is the way of the world. Put
your mask on. Hold my hand.

FIVE TRAVELLERS IN
A SMALL FORD

Iron Heinrich

there was a tenderness
in the lily pond
as the princess
leaned over her reflection
over the ripples of white silk
and suggestion

a tenderness as her soft
warm lips and her soft
warm breath came ever
closer, closer to the cold clamminess
of the frog's green forehead
his spawn-scented mouth

but her heart was not in it
she could not see ever after

Iron Heinrich saw it:
that's why he clanked
and clanked
and clanked
with laughter

Five travellers in a small Ford

Five travellers in a small Ford travelled across the Ardennes. The Hautes Fagnes. The High Fens.

The fifth traveller, strapped in a car seat, cried with hunger.

Clumps of cotton grass rose from the bog land on either side.

The car pulled off the road for the fourth traveller to nurse the fifth traveller.

The sky was grey and despite the late spring there were patches of snow in the shadows.

The third traveller puzzled at his mobile as the navigation system was awry.

Luckily, a signpost directed the travellers towards Eupen.

The second traveller, seated beside the third traveller, regretted not making muffins or packing fruit as, like the fifth traveller, the other travellers were hungry.

In 1940 Eupen was declared Judenfrei. Its citizens celebrated.

The first traveller sat in the shadows of a deserted stadium and put his notebook to one side.

He was a liar.

There was no fifth traveller, no fourth traveller, no third traveller and no second traveller.

This was ok. For this is fiction.

In 1940 there were no Jews in Eupen.

This was not ok.

This was not fiction.

Nina Simonestraat in Nijmegen

We never found it
except on the map:

a grey street
in a grey city
on the wrong
side of the highway.

In her red shoes
she would have walked
her anger down
to the river,

and then on
to the market:
potatoes, rutabagas
apples and pears,

ordinary fruit
from northern trees
very ordinary fruit
with strange names.

The muskrats at Versailles

He had been such a good boy forbearing before the faded
brocades, the gilt and galleries, the miles of mirrored aisles.

She'd felt an urge to pat his head as she'd patted the heads
of the marble busts just to spite their enigmatic smiles.

She'd half expected a crude *aperçu* when they found
the royal water closet, but he forbore there too

and she appreciated that. Above all he liked the doomed
queen's mill and millpond. This *nostalgie de la boue*

he far preferred to the king's unearthly symmetry,
golden means justifying geometry not art.

And she, being one who ever preferred the moon
to the sun, felt *simpatico* enough to take his part.

The pond was a milling mass of fish, of silver carp
with globular eyes and sucking, needy mouths.

He was delighted by their flurry, but their fury
sickened her and she felt the first seeds of doubt;

seeds which began to sprout when they saw the muskrats
(he called them *beavers*) basking on the grass:

large, fat, contented, black against the green. He loved them.
She hated them. She did not smile, she could not empathise.

These awful, graphic moments: the gulping carp, the muskrats,
her good boy—though not so good—and his unseemly kneeling at

fish and vermin so repelled her that all was all at once reduced,
traduced: the palaces, the stars, her love—to lazy beavers, rats.

Near the Bonner Münster

Seeing you swaying, strap-hanging
on the tram car, your hair still the colour
of straw and still reaching your
slender shoulders, I am suddenly

surprised once more how strange
the roads were that led you here,
how odd it is that we should all be
struggling still for balance together.

You are so street and cobble-stone
wise, so familiar with the oddness
of it all: the jugglers, the jongleurs,
the odours of wurst, fish and cheese.

The heads on the footpath do not
faze you: you even know their names
and where their bones are housed
and why and you smile and try

to explain—though all explanation
is lost in the silence of sightless
eyes, the wheeze of hydraulics
and the rattle of wheels on rails.

The Haribo factory

The scent of sugar everywhere
sweetens the street, the air
and we walk there as if the world
were fashioned from marzipan.

So good to walk the baby
in this honeyed world,
the warm ruffling wind
pink with cherry blossom,

but too seductive, of course:
for there are tonnes of hurtling steel
screaming nearby, and closer
a beeping warning the blind of traffic.

The factory stands four-square
on a corner. Its soft, warm breath
belies the cold precision with which
it slices, divides, weighs and numbers.

At Ravensbourne

the sea is chopped
and broken: white, grey
and all the shades between

out there is a small tugboat
with a blue wheelhouse
fighting the southerly home

now that our heaviness
has been discharged
there is finally air to breathe

and though the wind still blows
sharp and keen as buggery
the harbour still so far away

we can imagine ourselves
that lone macrocarpa on the far hill
holding up a lowering sky

as the heavy container ship
moves beyond the heads
and into the darkness

beyond the end of the passage
where there is a bedroom,
and beyond the bedroom
Rotterdam, Kowloon, Valparaiso

Promenade

The season is over,
the pleasure boats
tied up by the river,
the kiosks shuttered,
the gangways gated.

The wind off the water is cold
and will get colder.
In the shelter of the museum
bones and feathers do not move,

and nor do the bricks on the walls
the flags on the footpath.

But before their flesh falls
two men still walk,
arms draped about
each other's shoulders,
for a short distance
for a short time.

One looks like
Konrad Adenauer
the other looks
like another,
both heavily tattooed
by the weather.

Wasp at the trattoria

A small city on the table
of fluted glass and china
and this wasp-waisted
drone from nowhere
checking out the neighbourhood.

In shades, of course,
and a thorax to die for,
giddying himself with sauterne
and zagging in circles.

He is every interloper,
every gate crasher
cruising, swaggering,
predictable only
in his unpredictability.

The guests, even the host,
shrink into apprehension.

He has a phone.
He has friends.

Everything we love is frozen
suddenly date stamped,
temporary, on hold.

At Andrés Carne de Res

Red candles in the half-light,
hearts hang from the ceiling,
glasses shine through the steam
of a dozen bowls of soursop.

Creatures dangle above: a dusty
wolverine, a flying tiger both
watching the plates of battered
yucca being borne away

and making way (of course) for the solid,
solid flesh blessed by the solid cook,
flesh carried plattered to the table,
flesh peppered, sprigged and bleeding.

A glint of a serrated knife is in
his eyes as he admires the cut
of her, the rump and flank of her;
although her eyes, bevelled, remain oblique.

Together, they slice into the meat,
a red sea parting and she glimpses
the way ahead: her promised land
crated, paid for, carnal, red,

but only briefly, for here are
Pierrot whey-faced and smiling,
barefooted Columbine, and a man
with a white guitar offering to sing.

The knife

This is the knife we bought from Ikea
last trip. Beautifully designed. Swedish.

The black handle sits snugly in your hand
as if made for it, and the stainless blade

tapers elegantly to its point like a well-
crafted argument. I keep it very sharp,

so don't feel along the edge. Also from
Ikea we bought a sharpener: a three-

chambered, colour-coded set of emery
wheels that hone the blade to a razor.

I cut a lettuce at the stem for my lunch
and the bitter milk starts in small globules.

When I wipe the milk-stained blade
on my jeans I feel like a street fighter.

I carry the head to the kitchen and lay
it beside red tomatoes and bell peppers.

See how the knife slices through them: colour
opening to colour and colour and colour.

Reforestation in the living room

For too long this room has been plagued with bright light,
white wallpaper, suffered from a lack of branches.

How can the slow saucer-eyed loris hope to live here
while a peeping tom TV stretches and strains its iris?

Clusters of leaves would add shade, dapple and play,
water trickle. It would need only the flash and flicker

of birds, the march of ants, the fall of litter to re-carpet
the floor. Add humidity and the fine-spun heat could

wrap us in swathes of green silk, the orange tang
of gingerflowers, and the yelp of distant monkeys.

Books and magazines will turn brown and crinkle,
all angles become vines and corners bend into bends.

Sooner or later, of course, either the call of vinyl will drive
us back to the kitchen and the comfort of stainless steel,

or we must learn to lumber again like the slow-moving
pangolin, his proboscis swaying hopefully this way,

that way across the blotch, the splash of once-Axminster;
we must learn then to curl into the bracken-fern of sleep

and in that sleep the living room will breathe the deep breath
of the jungle; stretch, flex darkly, begin to feast on itself.

Notes to the poems

'Ziziphus': *Ziziphus jujuba* is a tree that bears small apple-like fruit, which are usually sold, sweetened and preserved, as Chinese red dates. We enjoyed these when we lived in China and, being a plant buff, I had long coveted a tree for our garden, but it was almost impossible to source in New Zealand. To my delight, I finally located and bought one. It died.

'Mycroft' references Sherlock Holmes's older brother, Mycroft.

'Hochstetter's frog': this frog is a rare New Zealand native species of a primitive frog family. It is under threat not only from introduced predators, but also from environmental degradation and disease.

'M. Hulot and the canary' references the Jacques Tati film *Mon Oncle* in which the character, M. Hulot, angles his window to direct sunlight onto a canary in a neighbouring apartment and thus encourages the bird to sing.

'Deadpan' references the wonderful Buster Keaton who, in one of his silent shorts, stands utterly unperturbed as the façade of a building comes crashing down around him. Keaton had worked out with mathematical precision that there would be an open window in the façade to slot over him and leave him standing unhurt as dust and chaos reigned about him. Apparently, the scene was not rehearsed. Keaton trusted his paper and pencil calculations.

'Telegraph Road' was prompted by the Canterbury earthquakes, in this case the quake of September, 2010. Telegraph Road stretches from the Main Road South (SH1) to Darfield in the west, and was close to the epicentre of the first big shake in 2010. I would not have found the displacement of the road here, though, as it occurred on nearby Clinton's Road.

'Iron Heinrich' references the Grimm brothers' tale *The Frog King or Iron Heinrich*, although it takes liberties with it. In the story, rather than kiss the frog, the princess hurls it against a wall. Iron Heinrich was the frog king's faithful retainer. It is a very strange tale.

'Nina Simonestraat in Nijmegen': Nijmegen is a small city in the Netherlands. For some time, Nina Simone lived in the city in self-imposed exile from an America she found increasingly racist and repugnant. There is a street named after her in the city.

'Near the Bonner Münster': the heads on the footpath in the poem are the large, sculpted, disembodied heads of early Christian martyrs Saints Cassius and Florentius, who were beheaded on or near the site. The heads are massive and children love to climb over them.

'The Haribo factory' is a confectionery factory in Bonn. Haribo is especially famous for its gummy bears.

'At Andrés Carne de Res' references a carnivore's delight: a restaurant in Bogotá, Colombia, with alarming but fascinating décor.

'Reforestation in the living room' is not entirely imagined. An eccentric late colleague of mine in Brunei, Borneo, once did attempt to create a jungle environment for a loris he had adopted; not a smart decision, really, given the slow loris has an extremely venomous bite and toxic fur. I preferred, as I often do, that the poem went elsewhere.

Acknowledgements

'Black-faced sheep' first published in *JAAM*

'Control tower' first published by *The Southeast Review* (USA)

'Crabmeat on the fifteenth floor' first published in *Fourteen Hills* (USA)

'Deadpan' first published in *Prole* (UK)

'Dear Messrs Smith & Wesson' first published in *Manifesto Aotearoa: 101 political poems*, edited by Philip Temple and Emma Neale, Otago University Press

'Five travellers in a small ford' first published in *Landmarks National Flash Fiction Day Anthology*, edited by Calum Kerr and Angie Holden, Gumbo Press, UK; subsequently published in *Bonsai: Best small stories from Aotearoa New Zealand*, edited by Michelle Elvy, Frankie McMillan and James Norcliffe, Canterbury University Press

'He had this thing' first published in *Pulp Literature* (Canada)

'Hochstetter's frog' first published in *Helix Magazine* (USA)

'The knife' first published in *London Grip* (UK)

'Last stop before Bethlehem' first published in *London Grip* (UK)

'Leaves' first published in *The Aurorean* (USA)

'Littoral' first published in *JAAM*

'The madness of crowds' first published by *The Hawaii Review* (USA)

'M. Hulot and the canary' first published in *Euphony* (USA)

'Mycroft' first published in *Jacket* (Australia)

'Naughty boys' island' first published in *Landfall*

'Near the Bonner Münster' first published in *International Poetry Review* (USA)

'Nina Simonestraat in Nijmegen' first published in *Australian Poetry Journal* (Australia)

'The poets at Makara' first published in *The Stillwater Review* (USA)

'Route 1003' first published in *Poetry Salzburg Review* (Austria)

'Scan' first published in *Acumen* (UK)

'scrim' first published in *Leaving the Red Zone*, edited by James Norcliffe and Joanna Preston, Clerestory Press

'Telegraph Road' first published in *Leaving the Red Zone*, edited by James Norcliffe and Joanna Preston, Clerestory Press

'The tennis ball' first published in *Salamander* (USA)

'There are times I feel like the egg' first published in *Green Hills Literary Lantern* (USA)

'Trumpet vine' first published in *Cordite* (Australia)

'Three times upon a time' first published in *London Grip* (UK)

'Underwear' first published in *Landfall* and subsequently in *Manifesto Aotearoa: 101 political poems*, edited by Philip Temple and Emma Neale, Otago University Press

'Wallet' first published in *Poetry Salzburg Review* (Austria)